PIBROCH

ALSO BY JOHN BOLLAND

Fallen Stock (Red Squirrel Press, 2018)

PIBROCH

John Bolland

To Imogen

with gratitude + warm wishes

John Bolland

RED SQUIRREL PRESS

First published in 2022 by Red Squirrel Press
36 Elphinstone Crescent
Biggar
South Lanarkshire
ML12 6GU

www.redsquirrelpress.com

Edited by Elizabeth Rimmer

Layout, design and typesetting by Gerry Cambridge
e:gerry.cambridge@btinternet.com

Cover image: Engineer studio/shutterstock.com

A CIP catalogue record for this book is available from the
British Library.

ISBN: 978 1 913632 29 8

Red Squirrel Press is committed to a sustainable future.
This publication is printed in the UK by Imprint Digital
using Forest Stewardship Council certified paper.
www.digital.imprint.co.uk

‘Cumha na Cloinne’ transcription by James MacDougall Gillies

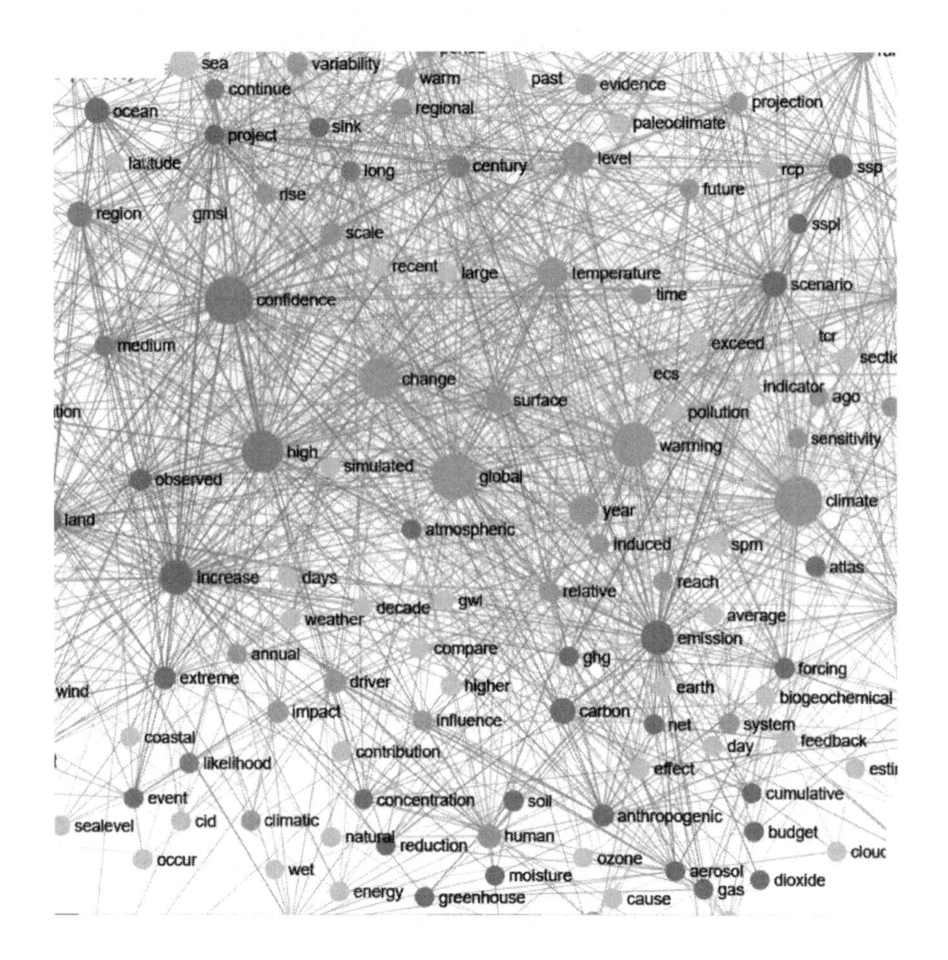

Discourse Structure Analysis

AR6 Summary for Policy Makers—IPCC 2021

AR6 Technical Summary—IPCC 2021

Contents

Urlar

‘Cumha na Cloinne’ transcription by Angus MacKay

Pibroch/Piobaireachd (also known as ceòl mòr) is a music genre characterised by extended compositions with a melodic theme and elaborate formal variations. Lament for the Children / Cumha na Cloinne is 'arguably the most beautiful lament, [and] is credited to Patrick Mor MacCrimmon after he lost seven of his eight sons within a year due to smallpox brought to Skye by a visiting ship'.

—The Piobaireachd Society

*

The Piper Alpha disaster, which occurred on the evening of 6th July, 1988, claimed the lives of 165 of the 226 persons on board and 2 of the crew of the Fast Rescue Craft of the Sandhaven whilst it was engaged in the rescue of persons from the installation. The death toll was the highest in any accident in the history of offshore operations.

In the weeks and months that followed, the bodies of 137 of the deceased were recovered from the wreckage of the East Replacement Quarters [ERQ], most of them in October and November 1988 after the ERQ had been raised from the seabed and transported to Occidental's terminal at Flotta in Orkney. 30 of the deceased remain missing.

On the morning after the disaster all that remained of the topside of the installation consisted of the wreckage of A-Module which contained the wellhead area. It took several days for a number of wellhead fires to be extinguished.

—The Public Inquiry into the Piper Alpha Disaster:
Chapter 2 Sections 2.1 to 2.3—HMSO 1990

You Watch the News

There was a large volume of evidence which indicated that the initial explosion occurred at, or within 1 or 2 minutes of, 22.00 hours BST. Some half dozen witnesses on the platform were listening to radio or television—some having just tuned in for the news or sports programmes. Some heard the 10 o'clock time signal, others did not. None claimed to have heard more than the very start of the news programme.

—Cullen Report: Volume 1 Section 5.14

You watch the news:
it's what we do.
Tune in. The water's on the boil

and all across this broadcast world, we
draw in power and generators kick
in, hum, air starters bark and flames ignite.
A whoosh of blue about the kettle's base.

But this one day

will not remain available upon-demand; no single day of

breathing
burning
living
loving
life

is ever so recorded.

What's on?
What's up?

Prayer desk is over, the weather forecast's fine. And now the
news…which does not mention

PSV504,
permit 2-3-4-3-4,
the fifteen tonnes of methane in the pipe.

This, after all,

is business as usual, new shift-same shit.
Like the blast on the Brents the night before,
the blast in the Voe on Sunday:
little flashes, little bangs out there in the oceanic silence as the sun,
at this moment,

22-01,

sets just for you.

Kitten Up a Tree

I am a kitten up a tree.
White west-coast Scottish working class and male and lucky.
Lucky: ay. A kitten up a tree.
A kitten? Me?

Late baby-boomer educated (sciences) the kind of schemie scruff
you drafted into economic growth and GDP—smart loon and
hungry. Desperate in fact. I kent the maths but naebdy ever tellt
me aboot gravity an vertigo an fear
$S=UT+\frac{1}{2}AT^2$ but what
a way
to fall?

Of course we take the drugs, the sugar, meds and petrol, the
hedonistic orgasm of arrival spilled into as many kids as we can
afford

if we keep climbing.

The only way is down.

That's gravity for you. And yet we climb precarious:
up through bills and branches, twigs and mortgages, expensive
habits, lazy choices, inertial marketing, wrong turns, egos
inflating like Montgolfier's balloon. Hot

air. 4-3-2-1. We have. Ignition.

Dodgy in a paper lantern. $CH_4 + 2O_2 \rightarrow CO_2 + 2H_2O$. But that's
not it.
That's it.
But that's not it.

Strikes match after match until the packet's empty.
Flicks them into the coal fire glowing in the grate.

Sweetness

Digesting other life, against its will,
diversified after the early Cambrian.
The violation probably started
with the tentacles of basal jellyfish.
Poisons permeated, points tore into flesh,
antler-picks prised ore, we learned to burn
and now the drill-string grinds
through sedimented time, releasing
the heat of Carboniferous afternoons
into our combustible Cockaigne. We can't
unlearn the comfort we derive
from warmth (or coolness), the thrill of speed,
the ease of traction powering the plough,
for we imagined it before in fairy fantasies and gardens
for the righteous. Ease and magic carpets:
ignoring the starving at the gate, zones of sacrifice,
the material reality of climate and terrain,
birth and death, violence and justice.
Like the tentacles of Cambrian jellyfish,
imagined power entangles us,
rendering life to stone once more.
Yet still we call this sweetness.

Lament for the Children—Urlar

In 1626...

Padraig McCrimmon's sons pass
from clan to meat and memory.
Smallpox.

Padraig's father, unforgiving,
burned some houses in Glenelg and killed
in vengeance for his brother's murder.
Who will avenge this massacre?

A prodigal returned, they say.
Sang at the ceilidh, prayed in the kirk.
Blameless.
            Infectious.
                        Plagued.
He died. So many died. His seven sons.
Seven out of eight.

It happens in strange weather.
Heat shimmers on Dunvegan Loch.
The burns run dry. Black cattle
cool themselves knee-deep in lochans.
Lose themselves in shade beneath the oaks.
Offshore, the busses bulge with maizies
mad to spawn but gill-caught, gutted, salted.
Barrels of dead herring
extracted and exported.
Ex.

He is the piper to the laird McLeod.
He shuffles notes
in lines of four.
  A B A B
  * A B A.

That silence is his namesake.
Padraig Og. His one surviving.
Scarred.
            Disfigured.
                        Death

in such fine weather is a wonder, is it not?
The world awash with fire, within, without.

Can you make melody
when 7 out of 8 tones are missing?
This is the beginning. 1626.
Sugar pans bubbling stirred
by plantation slaves.
Sweetness. Smoke.

Pump

To know and not to act is not to know
—Chinese proverb

In ten short generations we have learned
by rote to bleed enchantment from the well, to let it flow
through unseen veins—black and gross—
venting the in-breath of three hundred million years
in one disgusting fart

of affluence.

So, it is an inconvenient *thing*
to start again. A scunner really.

Black start from a stand-still when
we're busy pumping product to a quota and in any case it's what
we do: keep going,

shift after shift,
barrel by barrel,
pay-check by pay-check,
bonus at the year end.

And over there on the horizon?

They'll cope! They'll have it sorted, won't they?

The fire-pumps will kick in on cue, procedures will be followed:
gather at the muster points: await the next instruction

rescue
stand down
false alarm.

So we maintain back-pressure in the pipe,
till further notice, waiting for a sign—
even as we see the fatal glow.
Out there on the horizon.
Too far away to hear.
Out there
later
not now
somewhere else.

The eucalyptus trees catch flame.
The millet shrivels in the field.
The cat drowns in the cellar.

The day-shift guys did not survive.
The boys on shift that night
discovered gravity and jumped.

Shell Game, Aberdeen 1991

Years later, at a busy conference,
some smart-arse called us out. 'Hands-up! Who's read
the full report?' Fool, feeling fraudulent,
I cocked my wrist. We were full-speed ahead then,
turning trauma into profitable
opportunities, pontificating,
planning, spinning plates and comfortable
to piss about with ALARP[1] , PLL[2] .

But had we read the actual reports?
Hands up, now, children! Let's be honest.
The blindness of 'not-knowing' (yet) supports
fresh markets for delusion. Carbon-offsets,
guilt-free at point-of-sale, make you their shill,
ensuring Capital does not stand still.

[1] As Low as Reasonably Practicable
[2] Probability of Loss of Life

Mantra

You can't spend too much on safety.
You **can't** spend too much on safety
You can't **spend** too much on safety
You can't spend **too** much on safety
You can't spend too **much** on safety
You can't spend too much **on** safety
You can't spend too much on **safety**

Lost Time Incidents—Pithead

Aberfan—1966—146 Dead

She thought he'd take this lesson later in his life.
After a spell of vigour and delight, before the rigour
of hewn coal scarred flesh and lung too deep. Of course,
there is a tribal history of no goodbyes. The fire-damp flash,
the bells, the pithead waiting, waiting, waiting
for a corpse. But not, dear God! this suffocating
slurry so the boy was five parts coal before he was eight.

Letting Go

You hesitate. Sit in her armchair, pondering
whether this can wait?
Another glass? Another day,
as the old ones moulder in their lair?
Best get it over with. You start

with photographs and china ornaments, cut
glass swans you always loathed and loved.
From each, you wipe off memories
until the rag is saturated with regret.
Steal time deciding

what goes in the bin-bag,
what is set aside, still grasped too tight
though you know you cannot live with it.
Never wanted to, really. Memory
has no carbon footprint after all.

That done you pour another glass. The closets.
Dead-mink coat she never wore, holes
in the soles of his old shoes. Bottles, of course.
Empty as denial. Her underwear. Slam
shut that drawer. Later. Fabrics, laundry, crisp

creased table cloths she never used.
The empty bottles are the easy part:
no harm in one more then!
Mothballs spill on the rug like naptha-flavoured
pan-drops. Mummified! You laugh.

Resist
the urge to taste. The furniture sags
beneath black bags crammed with brogues
and pantsuits on their hangers, decades
to be carted off in a pretence of charity.

'Once upon a time'
they'd need these things. Grave goods.
They'd wait, composed, amidst this useless stuff and you
would have visited cobblers, laundromats, refilled
at least some of the bottles before you sealed

the place with blocks and curses. Why not?
You know their ways have no place here,
their time is now a tomb. You cannot own this
and survive. Press the cartouche into the lock.
Brick up all the windows.

Speculation

Cullen does not speculate on why the Navy turned up late.
(A Nimrod came and Rescue 1-3-8). Or why
the coast guard didn't call the polis back. You'll find no reference
here
to the melting point of rig-boots, random guess work, fatalistic
handshakes.

A Nimrod came that night and circled high. Heroically helpless
before the fire and fall, the bosuns watched the men above, in
contact with the searing steel,
test the melting point of rigboots, guess at random, bid farewell
and jump.
Heroic's not how it will be... for most of us.

Their palms in contact with the searing steel, survivors
scrambled through an atmosphere
combusting. Inexplicably reasonable, they clambered lower,
higher, higher still and jumped.
For most of us, that's not how it will be. Most of us will wait
complacently
upon instructions at the feeding station, trusting rescue will
come.

Inexplicably reasonable, the survivors fled across a warping web
of steel,
clinging to promises, suppressing shame.

While in the temporary refuge, the dying waited. Assured
someone would come.
Someone. They. They wouldn't let this happen. Would they?

Clinging to promises, suppressing shame, the disobedient few
survived.
Why wait upon instructions trusting? Why hand across your hope to
someone else?
Someone. They. Who let this happen.
Until the lights go out.
You wait and see...

We'll wait upon instructions as we're schooled to do,
guided by convention, expert opinion, corporate governance
until the lights go out. You wait and see...
They'll never speculate on why 'they' never came.

Philanthropy

Hijacked at 30,000 feet,
the milk of human kindness
is redirected to a remote
space-port in the Iberian desert.

Feckless goodwill thought
this trip would take them to the beach
and maybe a bit of culture.
But no—all sand, no sea, some tech.

The obsolete airliner waits
on an isolated runway as the desperate
philanthropists negotiate their terms. Amnesty,
more tax relief, a getaway rocket.

It is only a matter of time
before the passengers, hot and hungry,
storm the cockpit and overpower
the villains. Yes

there are casualties
but the passengers outnumber
the terrorists by 99 to 1.
Remember that.

Worst Case Scenario

The brief but brilliant atmospheric transit of the asteroid will
not be seen.
Nothing will hurt or disappoint.

The shockwave when the magma chamber bursts will not be felt.
Nothing will be funny and nothing will be sad.

The rumble of the tsunami will not be heard.
Nothing will be loved or laughed about.

The ash and sulphur in the air will not be tasted.
Nothing will be holy. Nothing will be true.

The stench of corruption will not be smelled.
Nothing will be mysterious or awesome. Nothing will be known.

Until it is again. Nothing.

Now jump!

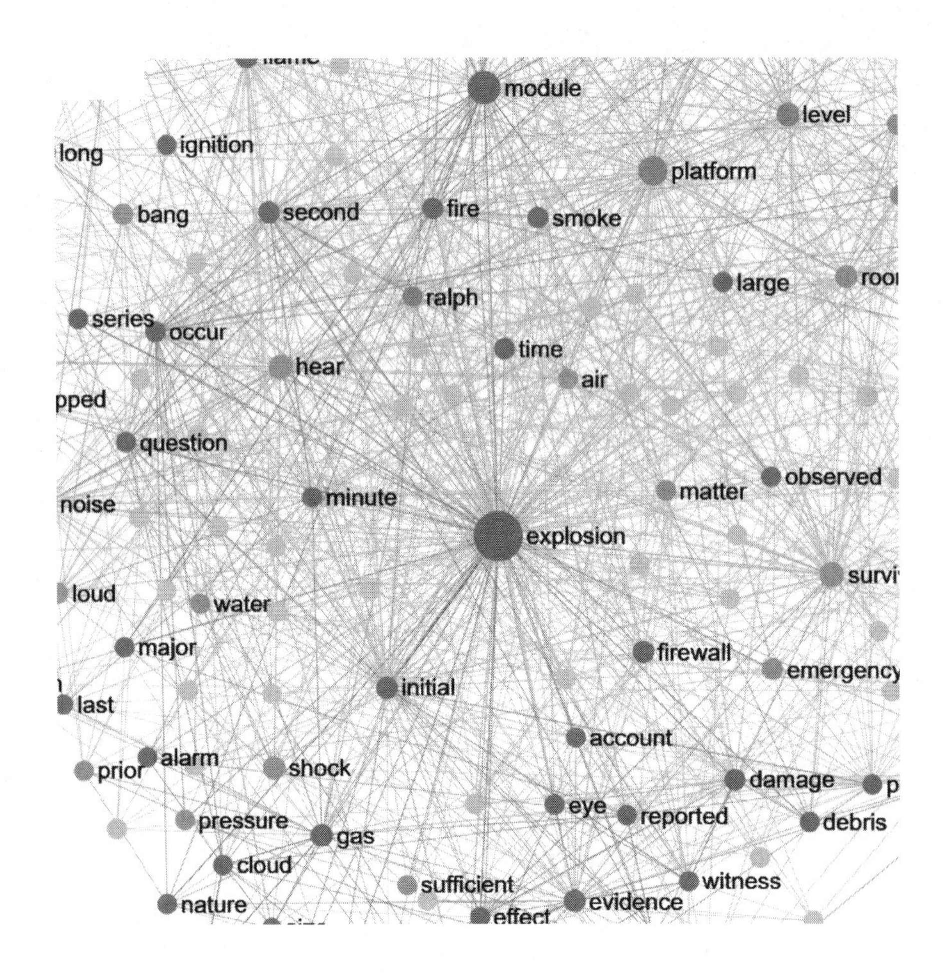

Discourse Structure Analysis
The Public Inquiry into the Piper Alpha Disaster:
Chapters 4–6—HMSO 1990

Dithis

'Cumha na Cloinne' transcription by David Glenn

Choke[1]

temperature,
pressure,
Jurassic
block 15/17
production,
NPV[2]
inventory,
Occidental
pump trip
BOPD[3]
PTW[4]
workshop
ROI[5]
handover
sandstone
Hammer

a whoosh
a muffled bang
the flare:
some lark
among the
scaffolders
a glimpse of a
flame
a scream
a banshee wail
tv news

22.01

shock
alarm
rupture
fireball
explosion
alarm
flame
overpressure
terror
panic
survival

burns
asphyxiation
grief
depression
guilt
drowning
addiction
back-pain
orphans
PTSD[6]
absence
memory
relief
evidence
enquiry
nightmare

[1]A choke valve is a type of control valve, mostly used in oil and gas production wells to control the flow of well fluids being produced.
[2]Net Present Value
[3]Barrels of Oil Per Day
[4]Permit to Work
[5]Return on Investment
[6]Post Traumatic Stress Disorder

...for millennia, human populations have resided in the same narrow part of the climatic envelope available on the globe, characterized by a major mode around 11°C to 15°C mean annual temperature (MAT). Supporting the fundamental nature of this temperature niche, current production of crops and livestock is largely limited to the same conditions, and the same optimum has been found for agricultural and non-agricultural economic output...in a business-as-usual climate change scenario, the geographical position of this temperature niche is projected to shift more over the coming 50 y than it has moved since 6000 BP... in the absence of migration, one third of the global population is projected to experience a MAT >29°C currently found in only 0.8% of the Earth's land surface, mostly concentrated in the Sahara.

—Future of the Human Climate Niche
Chu et al, PNAS 2020

We Listen to the News

We listen to the news:

it's what we do.
This chunked up sense embedded in white noise,
the bang crash clatter of catastrophe
bottles thrown off the stair-heid in a wally close.

In an average year.
Infernos erupt as havoc's wreaked
violence rips through crises of biblical proportions riven by the
force
of more and more and always more: chasing the dragon of the
worst,
the biggest-ever record-breaking costliest

unprecedented. In an average year.
Destructive power as blinding smoke casts tragic shadow
as if a bomb went off in a children's ward and new targets are set
for laser-guided ordinance whilst looting begins
amidst scenes of devastation and human tragedy.

In an average year.
Currencies collapse, prices double, electricity and bandwidth are
cut off, much needed food and water is everywhere or nowhere
to be found.
Unrelenting misery is heaped upon misery.
Stunning to look at.

In an average year
Tributes will be paid to those who stood no chance,
who'd long since learned to fear as hope began to fade
pushed to the brink defending homes reduced to rubble.
Fences will be built, more soldiers sent ensuring none escape.

Goldilocks

As I smoke the hive in careless PPE[1]—gauze mask and a pre-owned
smoker—my gloves
fail to avert the wrath of bees. Fair-dos. The stinging feels
just recompense for the callous plundering we resolved upon
before we bought the books on apiculture, this protective gear,
these frames and boxes capturing this hopeful tenantry
from which we garner rack-rent—wax and honey—
ignore their algorithmic disappointment,
leave a pittance and hope they'll go on pollinating.

My child will get the hang of this eventually
but presently she fears the frenzy of the guards enflamed
by pheromones that leak from martyrs' suicide-attacks.
'They're angry coz we take,' she says. 'We should not take.'

Yet still she'll gorge on stolen honey. I know
the queen is almost spent. The nurse bees mob the swarm cell
ready for secession. All through this Indian summer—
warmest spring—their drowsy buzz of pleasurably alive
implanted in each cell a female or a drone. But now
they make new queens.

Like Goldilocks, the little minx,
we've flourished in this zone of temperate sweetness where we live
abundantly—passing on the pattern. Kiss by kiss,
poems whispered mouth to ear. Your grandma's recipe, the taste of
sweets
at Eid revive our interrupted lyric for our children. Stotious revellers,
half-remembering the song but not the sense, we're blissed
by sugar squeezed from slaves, syrup sieved of othered life,
the honey in the comb.
'They're angry coz we take,' she says.
But will she take?

[1]PPE: *Personal Protective Equipment*

Lost Time Incidents—Kirkyard Hoast

Mesothelioma & Asbestosis—1968-1990—13,408 Dead

Sitting for years beside this scar that coughs
up coal and blood and phlegm
in constant re-confession of unconscious
error compounded shift by shift. Lungs
blackened by the facts of life. Raw
with the cost of fire or fire insurance.

Parable

They said they smelled the smoke while coming up the brae
and then they saw the flames. It was dark
by then.
Their tenement stood right up on the ridge. Great views
from their top floor flat. Enviable:
all that light
and air when neighbours only got the windows opposite.
'Safe as houses'—that's still what they say—
and the eldest was in with them—he was nine.
And they said the lights were off
and the three of them were sleeping when they left
and this new natural gas is safer than the gas they had before
and they said it was only for the one and the other thing, the
Conroys turning up,
was unforeseen and they said, 'You don't know how steep that
brae is
until you have to run.'
And they said the fire engines didn't come
till later
and, of course, they hoped it was the close next door
and they said the eldest boy could reach the sneck
if he stood up on a chair
and she should have turned the gas off and he should have called
it a night
and you'd think someone would notice do something—raise the
alarm!
And I know I could have been different
and you know you shouldn't have done it
and we know we should have
could have
should

That's what it'll be like.

Testimony

I looked across and I could see my mates across on this other leg and I thought 'Right good, I'll come back that way again and I'll go round and I'll get them' and as I made my way up there was another explosion and they too were engulfed—they were incinerated and burnt. See your first emotion then is one of relief. It's terrible. Coz you know that could have been me. Then you've got the guilt and a terrified feeling comes over you again.

—Bob Bannatyne, *The Night I Almost Died*

In your telling (when you tell) you're always climbing jumping
swimming
folding the flashing scraps of raw remembering
trying to pin
an ember back into the burning night yawing and slipping on this
melting
thing that's always happening this thing happening groaning
through dreaming sweating-cold amazing that your darling sleeps
oblivious
to the distance that you're falling
falling arriving sinking drowning
surviving floating on the promise of a wedding recalling
a laughing loving woman waiting hoping. Ninja-like
still clinging to the searing steel or clawing at the rocking rib
energised by terrifying noise. Surviving
again and again surviving again then waking crying living not
dying. Scarring healing into binging
lost weekends lost moments gin relieving grieving. Not
missing. Forgetting. Then bingo! Glimpsing
someone gesturing just so though you've seen him
disappear into the roaring. Everything flooding back
paralysing realising you were memorising every choking, gasping,
scorching
moment while turning thinking deciding praying helping always
pushing shoving climbing jumping swimming living crying
in your telling.

Lament for the Children—Dithis

Meanwhile in 1628...

(The physics never changes for there is no time.)

Viewed from the pitching birlinn on An Cuan Sgith,
Eilean a' Cheò dissolves and Innse Gall
precipitates out of the winter squall,
grainy under Roineabhal. But it is you
who travel from nostalgia towards a different shore:
though every ache and whimper, every blurring tear, caress,
bramble stain, skint knee and milk tooth, giggle,
mischief, kindness and reproach were real and will be real,
though entropy pays out the tow of time,
binds you to what's lost, ensnares you in what will be lost
(for there'll be losses yet). McCrimmon sails
towards his dead sons' future though already in their past
and Padraig's future griefs are real and inconsolable
though not yet now—or merely overlooked. Ceol mor
as hair-shirt and as valediction. St. Clement's tower
at Roghadal.

Confidence

8.8 In the event the system was almost entirely inoperative and little command or control was exercised...

—The Public Inquiry into the Piper Alpha Disaster:
Chapter 8 HMSO 1990

Dad is wearing a survival suit.
He must know.
He does not have a radio.
He does not ask to use the public address system.
He leaves for his private bunker without giving further instructions.
Dad takes no initiative in an attempt to save life. Perhaps not even his
own.

All Dad says is: 'evidence work control module alarm.'

Five minutes later he comes running back in a state of panic.
Surely by then he knew.
After that there is confusion delirium commotion heckling.
Dad slumps down trying to calm everyone, saying,
'The whole world knows we are having problems.'
So he knew. He does not seem able to come up with any answer.
No one takes charge.

At this point, Dad says, 'attribution adaptation mitigation pathways
governance systems scenarios.'

The personnel—the boys and girls, the women and the men,
the mothers, fathers, brothers, sisters, sons and daughters wait
in the mess. Some of them
will decide they have to find a way out. Some will wait
in the hope of rescue. Some will leave because
there is no point in staying. Some have stayed because they have been
told

to wait. Some take the view that they have nothing to lose. Some simply don't know what else they can do.

But all Dad says is, 'private finance sustainable option industrial sequestration future equilibrium ecosystem services weather security human investment indicator billions the fuck the fuck
the fuck.'
There is no systematic attempt to lead us to a means of escape.
A large number make no attempt to leave. The risks of death are
considerable.
Those who remain in expectation or obedience will succumb
to the effects of smoke and gases. That is what happened—last
time.

Dad will never mention: funerals melting engulfing guilt
drowning nightmares loss compulsion mates distress grief
starving mum shouting rape addiction exile prison rescue
youngest grandchild remorse
loneliness
denial
incineration
pain...

All That's Humanly Possible...

He seems to be determined to do the best he possibly can in the circumstances.
—Memo to PM Margaret Thatcher: Dominic Morris 15/7/88

I was grateful for you coming over
We are doing everything humanly possible to help those who have suffered.
so soon after the tragedy,
Yesterday I arranged that the Occidental Consortium will pay
for your ready grasp and understanding
the contracting companies the cost incurred by them of payments to any employees unable to be deployed to other work.
of what was required,
The employees involved will be retained on their standby rate according with their existing contract of employment.
for the warm humanity and generosity
This agreement will remain in place till 31st December 1988.
you have shown then and since.

Note: *Found poem based on the texts of CEO Dr. Armand Hammer's note to Margaret Thatcher of July 1988 and her response.*

Fetch

The fluid
world convects,
subducts
as the gyre of six
sextillion tons of rock
birls it around
and round again
to warm beneath the sun
then chill in shadow.
Winds and currents,
waves and rain stir leaves,
stir kelp, stir
turbines' blades
as forests gulp down air
and generators hum
and we gaze out
across the fetch,
learning to love
the flow and not
the fire.

Teach Your Child to Swim

Teach your child to swim.
Though those skills might seem implausible
in a desiccated landscape whose only river,
glacier fed, is full of crocodiles.

Teach your child to swim.
Though the family lore insists
it only prolongs the agony: the cold
will kill you anyway.

Teach your child to swim.
Though you live in pleasant suburbs
in Barcelona, Athens, Dallas or LA.
For fire and flood is coming.

Sooner or later.

Our children will confront the River Styx
and find the ferries cancelled
and the coasts patrolled.
Teach your child to swim.

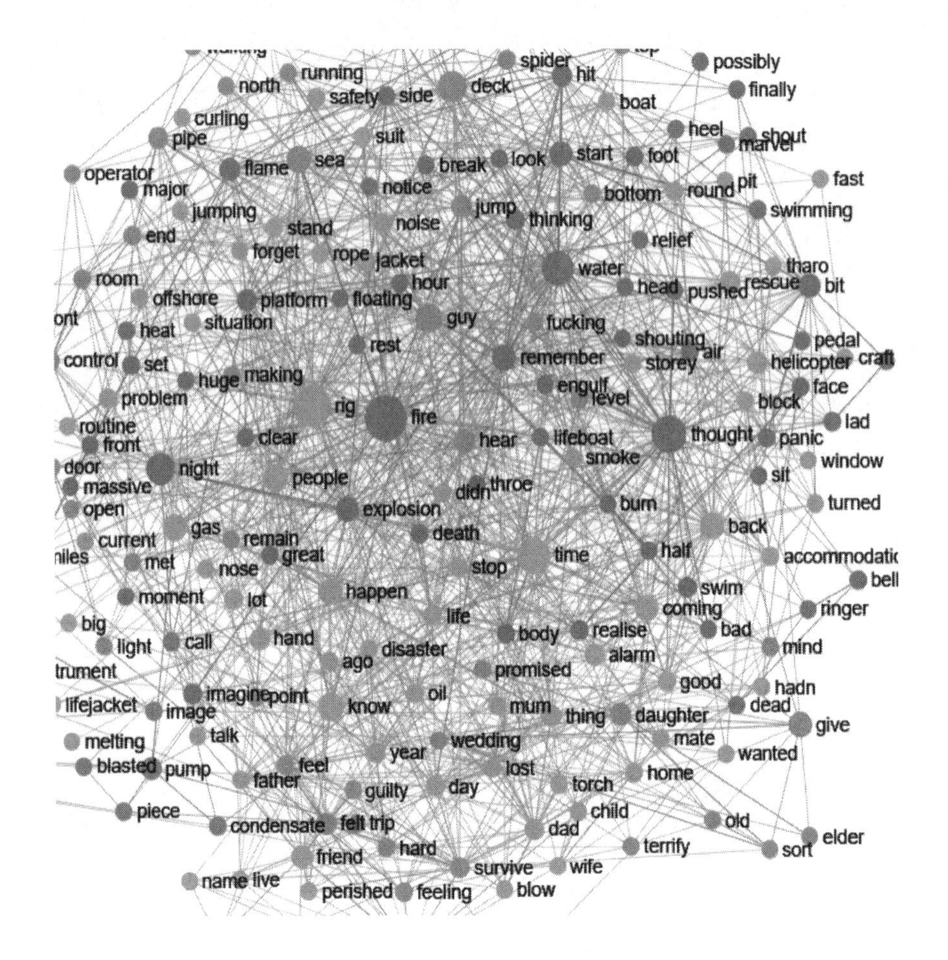

Discourse Structure Analysis

Piper Alpha Survivors & Relatives—Public Testimony

Siubhal

‘Cumha na Cloinne’ transcription by Donald MacDonald

Choked

combustion burns
extraction starvation
Carboniferous grief
freedom drought shifting seasons depression
production wildfires terror guilt
Capital flooded homes ice-loss drowning
GDP[1] growth violence hunger poverty
entanglement starving bears thirst incarceration
greenhouse effect warm winters 2021 misery orphans
violation bleached coral heat-stroke mass extinction
speed migration homelessness silence
RCP[2] food aid methane releases memory
mobility storm-surges panic dislocation
hydrocarbon rape survival despair
sweetness blame
deep time nightmare

[1]Gross Domestic Product
[2]Representative Concentration Pathway

This is how one pictures the angel of history. His face is turned toward the past. Where we perceive a chain of events, he sees one single catastrophe which keeps piling wreckage upon wreckage and hurls it in front of his feet. The angel would like to stay, awaken the dead, and make whole what has been smashed. But a storm is blowing from Paradise; it has got caught in his wings with such violence that the angel can no longer close them. This storm irresistibly propels him into the future to which his back is turned, while the pile of debris before him grows skyward. This storm is what we call progress.

—*Theses of History IX*
Walter Benjamin

I Watch the Forecast

I watch the forecasts:

This is what I do.

As if in need of telling it has rained for weeks,
the cellar's full of water, the garden's silent and the cats are gone.
Forecasters blur the truth in facts,
in logs and axes: earnest men in dayglo life-preservers seeking
firm ground as they tread deep water,
never daring to swim,
not yet. They phrase the flood and fire as

food insecurity or loss of ecological services,
burden of disease or economic risk,

quantifying the bloody obvious, ignoring
the soon to be extinct elephants in the room:

anthropogenic forcing: indigenous knowledge: sacrifice zones.

Policy-makers calibrate catastrophe (with varying degrees of confidence)
in years and decades, centuries with margins for error ignoring
long-tail effects,
framed (for the purposes of governance)
in the capitalist hoax of objective time. Whilst we
thrive and suffer in moments, seasons, generations, lifetimes, cultures:
never calling this thing out for what it is—this *thing* that's
happening now.
This *thing* that is our fault. A *thing*. A fault. That's happening.
Only that.

I watch the forecasts:

That is what I do.

Lost Time Incidents—Quayside

Trawler deaths—Scotland 1945–2020—502

You watched from shore—they foundered on the reef—
a queer cathartic awfulness close but never close enough:
the North Sea has no sense of proportion. The beach
is patient. Others know the numbness of the empty berth.
The rumour of a capsize somewhere far. Wet fish
sloshing in the hold. Imagine the overwhelming.

It Does Not Care

it does not care
the pressure in the pipe
the agitated molecules
the crystal conformation
the gap

it does not care
the fugacity of the fluid
the pressure differential
the energy of exothermic reaction
the spark

it does not care
the coefficient of expansion
the index of congestion
the yield strength of the fire wall
the blast

it does not care
the decibels, the vapour pressure, mix
the interrupted conductive path
the force of gravity
pool fire

it does not care
the rupture point of skin cells
the bonding energy of monoxide in the blood
the hoop strength of the riser
irradiated

it does not care
the terminal velocity
surface tension of brine
specific density of oil
angle of approach
falling

the sustained back pressure in the line
the lack of preparation and planning
the insistence on keeping plant online
the poor design, lax standards
failure to attend:
for those there's no excuse.

Survivors

I was really in a bad way, then I thought, 'I'm either going to burn to death or be drowned.'

And I said, 'I think I'd sooner drown. I think that's a more peaceful death.' And I plunged myself under the water and pedalled down under the water and thought I was maybe going under for the last time. I got an image of my younger daughter and I had promised to give her the same sort of wedding I had given my older daughter and this sort of clicked with me and I said, 'I have got to survive this.'

—Roy Carey, Instrument Technician, *Piper Alpha*

The sea is deep
and cold and full
of counter-currents, terrors, implacable suffocation. You cling
to this rubber rib, mouth barely proud of the meniscus of your
hopes. Your child gripped by the collar, floats face down. Futile
life-jackets surface husks and hulks, rejected by the density of the
moment.

Behind you now the heat,
the thirst, the smoke.

The mangling of hyper-ordered space: quotidian, reliable.
Sound. Its sundering groans are heard (they say) above the sound
of hell.
The molten twist of the predictable, the roaring of a kidnapped
Earth venting grief and disappointment. Desperate hope.

Behind you
the desert,
the minefield,
the maze.

No purchase

on this rib for hands, the whorls and scars and callouses of
identity slough away. On contact.
Fortuitous
for a future in which you are not yourself. Undocumented (though
a news item) huddled in the piss-stained doorway of a new world.

Heroically,

a coxswain grabs you by the hairs which wave like wrack beneath
an oily swell.
You're sinking but you're caught. His fingers
scraping your scalp to wrench the last thoughts from your
humming.

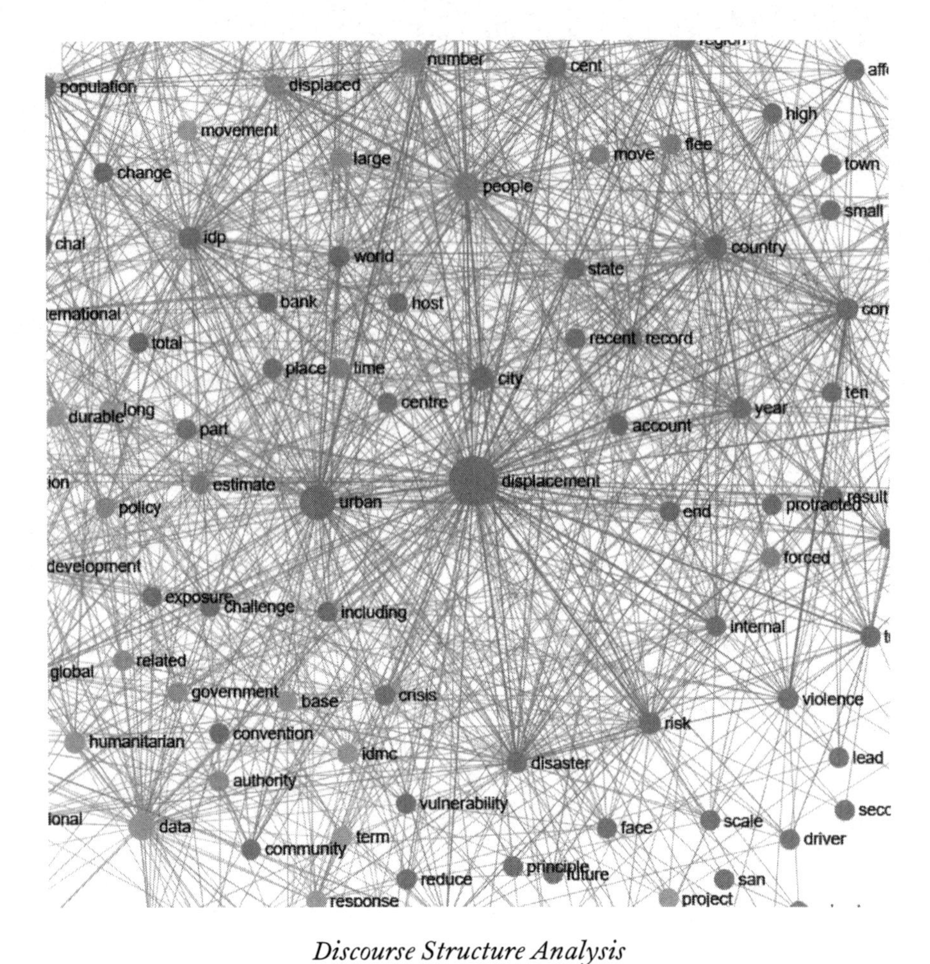

Discourse Structure Analysis

Global Report on Internal Displacement 2019—IDMC

International Migration 2019—UN Dept of Economic & Social Affairs

Christenings

He went to all the ceremonies, afterwards, and that was hard,
the hardest thing to say:
that you lived while their bairns would not;
bearing the how and when and where of it
in a scorched fire blanket of evasion and apology. Silence mostly.

Why
share the horror of what you know with those for this moment
shielded, locked-down in their innocence
of physics, indolence and greed—the sheer incompetent three ring
circus everyone assumes
is local not global,
personal not general,
exceptional not my circus,
not my monkeys. But they are.

Time and again
he watched them sprinkle water on the baby's head:
remembering the deluge system failed.
Swallow 100-proof oblivion: salt on the tongue like drowning.
Cross the fragile skull with ash and oil
like a tree marked to fall
like a house full of plague. No but
Hope! Pandora's curse.
No not that: Hope!

Is a butterfly emerging soggy from the arse of the angel of history.

Optimism of the will—that schtick—has him accosting
wedding guests and godparents,
school teachers, policemen, priests.
mothers and fathers. Siblings. Look!
Somewhere else a wild fire is burning
the parched earth is starving

the bombers are circling
the long trek continues
the furniture's floating
your grandma is gasping
for breath. I mean:
who'd have a christening under these circumstances?

But we do. Welcome. It's the first word that springs to our lips
unless
you're the bad fairy at the feast
forbidding her from shooting at the fucking scurries
warning her about needles and the ways of men
unable to explain exactly why but knowing it's a curse.
After all you've been through.
Just don't.
Or else.
Really

Biospheres

This analysis therefore showed that the pressures required to destroy both the B/C and C/D firewalls, 0.1 and 0.12 barg, respectively, were less than most of the values estimated for the maximum peak over-pressure caused by the initial explosion.

—The Public Inquiry into the Piper Alpha Disaster:
Chapter 5 Section 5.102—HMSO 1990

Despite this, humans themselves are too numerous, widespread and adaptable to be at serious risk of extinction any time soon. It is far more likely that we will extend our distribution yet further by engineering habitable biospheres on other planets.

—Matthew Wills, Professor of Evolutionary
Palaeobiology at the Milner Centre for Evolution
University of Bath

A subterranean penthouse beneath the Kansas Prairie
costs 4.25 million dollars—full planning permission—cash only.
Video feeds will fill your windows with the time of day and
shopping
is encouraged as a socialising process. Self-contained
and self-sufficient survivalists can wait for the PAW—
the post-apocalyptic world—their cars still parked outside,
the prairie grass still blowing, the security-guard (long gone)
still idling at his post.
Alas: all units in the first geoscraper
are already sold: more in the pipeline.

Alternatively—Mars with Elon Musk might cost you half a
million.
Ticket only: accommodation not (yet) included.

In the meantime—fences, walls and gate-keepers
patrol ships, killer drones, incarceration. Invest
not in your own future comfort—but crowdfund the other.
Think in terms

of borders, firewalls, demarcations,
us and them. Cordons sanitaires, red lines, track and trace. The
world

conceived as barriers. This: not this. This
has been tried. Blast-walls. Water-tight
bulkheads. Air gaps. Alarm systems.

The pressures released in that giving moment,
the over-pressures shaped by inconsiderate design,
the functional congestion of the space,
the jewellery and the scaffolding,
that force
will tear through every wall that you imagine
as if it was and is imaginary.
Shards of what you thought protected you
will puncture you and slice through veins, the conduits
that vitiate your world. Bees will sing like shrapnel:
biota you never thought to care about
metamorphose to shards of flying glass.

Growth

Of course, things change. Things
always change. After the burning years,
the splitting years, the pulping years, first one
and then another presence reappears as branches
burgeon, leaves glut, roots reach out
to mycorrhiza whispering news of need and opportunity.
We offer solace, offer aid. We puzzle out
some dialects we had forgotten, recovering
meaning through the sizzling persistence of mycelia.
Kith and kin
flourish in the thickened air. Mothers
foster stands before new storms, pass on
rich legacies then rot
back, repeating and repeating. All things
interknit and slowly fix imbalance
back into the rock.

Lament for the Children—Siubhal

On Innse Gall...

The pibroch needs lost time to make its harmonies
proceed from memory to anticipation
across the fragile bridge of one
particular configuration of eight digits
and a constant pressure on the bag.

Nine tones and four phrases
He locks the pattern into memory like spin-cells
evolving from experience—DNA transcripted
amidst trial and error—heuristics and tradition.

Grace notes and doublings, tachums and birls
encrust like beardy mussels, trail like kelp—
reminiscences slowing the steady tread of the Urlar,
the steady progress of lament celebrating
present absence

and coming absence present just the same
until the chanter's broken and the drones
proscribed—the tongue's forbidden:
headstones mumble in the mist like puirt à beul.

Ignition

'It wiz fry or jump. So we jumped.'
A. Mochan. *BBC News 7th July, 1988*

Not yet.
Jist wait.
I'm doin this.

And then...

I will.
When I get free of this.
I'll

do it. Honestly.
I've just to get
Where?

Just around the next
corner, over the next
ridge. Through

this. Set the world
to rights. Expunge
past wrongs.

Assuage my guilt
by demonstrating theirs.
Make them

confess to this. That's
worth the effort
and delay.

Hurry up, I'm on fucking fire here!

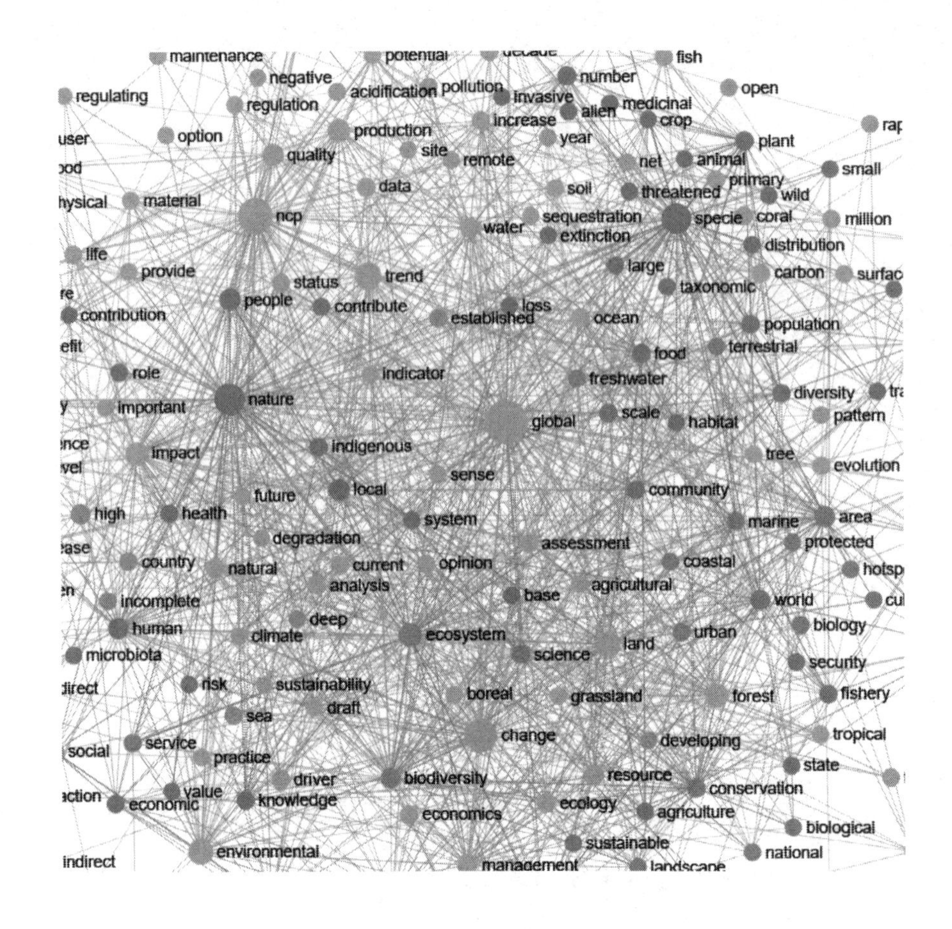

Discourse Structure Analysis

Global Assessment of Biodiversity and Ecosystem Services—IPBES 2019

Taorluth

'Cumha na Cloinne' transcription by Uilleam Ross

Unchoked

combustion flow
extraction moderation
Carboniferous circularity
freedom drought justice mutuality
production wildfires compassion hospitality
Capital flooded homes ice-loss education
GDP[1] growth violence creativity community
entanglement starving bears decisiveness bee-buzz
greenhouse effect warm winters 2021 Jubilee joy fructation
violation bleached coral imagination cherishing
speed migration shifting seasons bird-song
RCP[2] food aid resilience memory
mobility storm-surges migration belonging
hydrocarbon rape survival balance
sweetness nurture
deep time deep time

[1]Gross Domestic Product
[2]Representative Concentration Pathway

Populations at disproportionately higher risk of adverse consequences with global warming of 1.5° C and beyond include disadvantaged and vulnerable populations, some indigenous peoples, and local communities dependent on agricultural or coastal livelihoods (high confidence). Regions at disproportionately higher risk include Arctic ecosystems, dryland regions, small island developing states, and Least Developed Countries (high confidence). Poverty and disadvantage are expected to increase in some populations as global warming increases; limiting global warming to 1.5° C, compared with 2° C, could reduce the number of people both exposed to climate-related risks and susceptible to poverty by up to several hundred million by 2050 (medium confidence).

—IPCC Special Report—Global Warming of 1.5 Degrees,
Section B.5.1 (2018)

Listen

Listen...
My Dad worked constant night-shift twenty years
of eight-till-eight six days a week maintaining
production in a soulless place they called a car-plant.
The isolation of that...working through the dark
to keep the wheels on...

Imagine.

Isolated as a blue planet in the well of space
the installation hums as it sinks beneath the horizon
sucking centuries of photosynthesis out of the rock:
black sludge and bubbles.

22.01

Carnoustie's
in the tea shack and Crieff is in the gym. Polmont's
gone to check the pump, Vancouver's in his bunk
though not yet gone to sleep. And Hartlepool and Sheddocksley
and West Kilbride and Fergusson are tinkering and Bradford's
in the lab.

Each in their personal space
these soon-to-be-a hole-in-someone's-life
breathe, itch, sweat, zone-out, tease, worry,
fantasise, concentrate. Sleep. Dream.
Digest. Remember. Ache. Wait.

And in a moment
their waiting will wait—forever—missing

in Aberdeen, Peterhead, Insch, Kirkcaldy, Inverurie, the Broch,
Stranraer, Dundee, Larbert, Fleetwood, Cleveland, Leith,
Banff, Rancon, Middlesbrough, Coatbridge, Roker, Navasota
Texas, Lossiemouth, Portlethen, Arbroath, Peterculter,

Cumbernauld, Keelby, West Kilbride, Greenock, Hartlepool, Tain,
Buckie, Carnoustie, Nigg, Bridge of Don, Cove Bay, The Wirral,
Elgin, Billingham, Ardrossan, Greenock, Sunderland, Nairn,
St Helens, Brechin, Rotherham, Port Seton, North Shields, North
Kessock, South Shields, Linlithgow, Warrington, Wallsend,
Wallasey, Pitlochry, Reading, Llanwit, Wemyss Bay, Cumbernauld,
Blyth, Saltburn, Edinburgh, Broughty Ferry, Stockton, Bridgton,
Dalgety Bay, Sheffield, Alness, York, Hurlford, Torry, Stepps,
Clydebank, Turriff, Woodside, Stafford, Raploch, Saltcoats,
Dalkeith, Kirkwall, Rosyth, Belfast, Oldmeldrum, Bucksburn,
Grangemouth, Neilston, Milltimber, Sheddocksley, Urmston,
Bromborough, Inverurie, Hayes, Roseburn, Linlithgow, Polmont,
Findochty, Gellilydan, Crieff, Largs, Polmont, Westhill, Thirsk,
Vancouver, Buckhurst Hill, Montrose, Uphall, Maryhill, Hessen,
Bieldside, Sandhaven, Grimsby, Ellon, Hull, Mintlaw, Montgarrie,
Peterborough, Glenrothes, Danestone & Highbury.

Note: *The poem lists the hometowns of the 167 men who died on Piper Alpha on the night of the 6th July 1988.*

Lazarus Taxon

Life goes on. The question is

whether you want to be a subject of history
or
some prehistoric, post-historic object peered at by something that
evolved out of an arthropod or a mollusc?

On scientific paper your individual odds as you slip into and through
this 6th mass extinction are better than most.

According to the literature, successful applicants for the next epoch
should be:
adaptive,
eurytopic,
a complex generalist with a range of opportunistic strategies,
located near potential refugia.
LUCKY!!!!!!!

And typically we are. Provided we are white.

On the downside:
Our reproductive cycle is too long.
Our size demands significant resources to sustain life.
Despite their best efforts...we can't eat shit.
Our larval phase is not resilient to extended periods of
environmental stress.

We burn too easily,
drown too easily,
starve too easily,
break too easily,
suffocate too easily.

But you might survive.

In mid-to-high latitudes in gated, biospherical communities
subsisting on the ersatz synthetic artificial and comprehensively
monetised,
providing you have resilience, adaptability, courage or
substantial liquid assets at this time. On the other hand,
if you don't know how to grow your own or kill your own,
build a shelter or have several million in the bank in RCP8.5,
you'll probably wish you were a mollusc or an arthropod.

The Last Haul

10.4 On 4 August the British Magnus was demobilised in order to proceed to her original work for BP. On 8 August the Seaway Condor, a diving support vessel, took up the survey work which had previously been done by the British Magnus. As from 10 November 2 fishing vessels, the Heather Sprig and the Janeen were used to trawl in a wider area for debris and any human remains which had not been located previously. Arising out of this work, 4 bodies were recovered between 15 August and 17 October; and a further 6 between 31 October and 22 November 1988

—The Public Inquiry into the Piper Alpha Disaster:
Chapter 10—HMSO 1990

Bodies already float in this place ungoverned:
midwater or weighed down,
among the pipelines, wrecks, lost tackle, neutrabuoyant
polystyrene cups drifting in the wake of cancelled ferries:
until they rise again, surface out of sight
in this international nowhere
unmanned
by gentlemen's agreement.

What are you going to do about it?

Bake bones dry between
grim caravanserai of razor wire and portacabin
boredom and abuse contracted out
to client states?

Ensure what happens
in Mosul and Idlib, Darfur and Delta, Oromia, Borno, Ar Raqqa, Kirkuk,
Sebha, Rakhine, Odisha, Ninewa, Herat, Vanuatu, Putumayo, Kasai
stays locked-down in Mosul and Idlib, Darfur and Delta, Oromia, Borno, Ar Raqqa, Kirkuk,

Sebha, Rakhine, Odisha, Ninewa, Herat, Vanuatu, Putumayo,
Kasai,
as temperatures and tempers, water levels

rise, survivors climb up and up through their predicament
looking for refuge,
somewhere to jump off,
another place to thrive?

What happens
as each year fence-lines drift
up through the latitudes, contours and isotherms,
ratcheting misery—one degree, two degrees, three degrees, five
till what happens in Paradise, Ballater, Piave, Benbecula, Cape
Fear and Galveston,
Canberra, Sydney, Sonoma, New York, Shanghai, Mumbai,
Miami, London
is locked down in...you take my drift.
When it's you that is clambering up and up through your
predicament?

What are you going to do about it?
When?

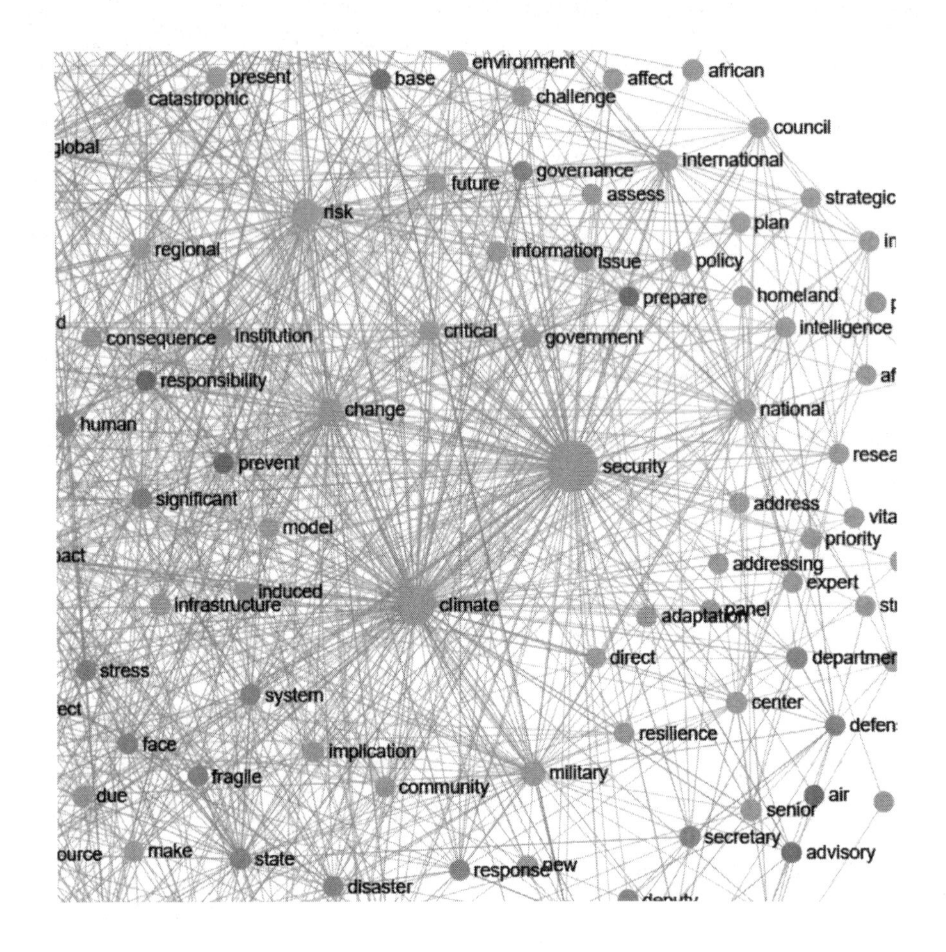

Discourse Structure Analysis

The Responsibility to Prepare & Prevent: A Climate Security Governance Framework for 21st c. —2019

A Security Threat Assessment of Global Climate Change—National Security, Military & Intelligence Panel on Climate Change 2020

A Climate Security Plan for America—The Climate Security & Advisory Group 2019

Lost Time Incidents—Infirmary

Workplace fatalities not related to 'disasters'—1940–1990—69,770 Dead

He never should have gone so high,
so close or touched the terminal or
climbed aboard. He should have listened
for the train. He should have said
before he went about his business, kissed
the bairns a last farewell each & every morning.

Mean

It is time to complete the defeat
of porcine profiteers who feed
on obscene greed they breed
from marketeers who steer with dreams and memes insisting on
our need for gasoline,
adrenaline and saccharines—
project onscreen hypnotic scenes false freedoms schemes that
contravene
our basic human decency. In this Anthropocene
we still bleed, breed and raise from seed the staples that we eat,
glean meaning from defeat and all the while our feet
march to the beat of their machines.
Overseen by sub-routines. Big data overweens. The sheen
of kerosene floats on once pristine surfaces while submarine
microplastics choke and genes mutate. Greens fade in heat.
And internecine conflict follows famine.
We need
to heed the bonfires of this Pyrocene and lead,
as lithic alkenes weep and seep from wells,
leak from exhausts and landfill overseen
by racketeers and libertines who sell false need
like methamphetamine. Labyrinthine chains
of cause-effect reach back into the Pleistocene.
We've never seen these temperatures before
It's never been so hot. We've never been so vulnerable.
Eight billion of us! Time to queer
the pitch. Be mutineers. Refuse. Re-engineer and commandeer
our future. For our children.

Call it what it is: CAPITALOCENE.

Lament for the Children—Taorluth

Puirt à beul still echo in the fog
around the stones at Callanish.
Past griefs congeal to runes and ogham:
tattoos trace lineage, knots of remembering.
All our heads are wetted by this sea road.
Each tongue will taste the salt and yet
the future will have music:
the tread and snap of fingers, voices
mobilised by hope and joy and tears.
New life, new steps, new cadences.
There will be change, the trees insist,
but still we'll birl in time
and gift and get and ceilidh. The world
cannot do otherwise.

In Time

First we let us in.
It seemed so obvious though unpredictable
in consequence: for who
are we? Who us? And then

we ripped out all
the fence-lines, toppled dykes. We had to make
fast travel a taboo as stirks
wandered the highways. Hogs

agreed a wary truce. Bracken
suffered, nettles throve and comfrey. Of course,
there was some hunger. It was
shared. Shorn ewes grazed
amongst the salad greens. Electricity

was taken when available. Conversation
flourished
and fructated, debating
what to read and whether
not to. Luthiers
and poets, healers, dowsers,
foresters and engineers

were all the rage. Everyone grew
something. There were
no call centres. No one
waited on the next available nothing
was insured assured. We learned

to dance, forgave their debts and accepted
obligations, offered
more or less, were kind
as barren cities emptied. Burned
deeds and contracts every Jubilee until
no slaves remained. Infants

decided not to be born. Elders withdrew. Kith
proliferated. We were less-many. We/us
became a favoured pronoun. There-their-they
withered in the heat. Then were
no surpluses: only trees

and seasons. We travelled in increments, traded
kilogrammes not tonnes,
foraged in gardens, worked
with the forest, the rivers, the sea.
We welcomed

the rain and we were not distracted. We chose
to listen not to fly. Knowledge was
common knowledge and ingenuity was
effervescent. Eventually

we let the earth forget us,
our fossils rare as hens' teeth
above the thin black line we traced
in time but cut
in time.

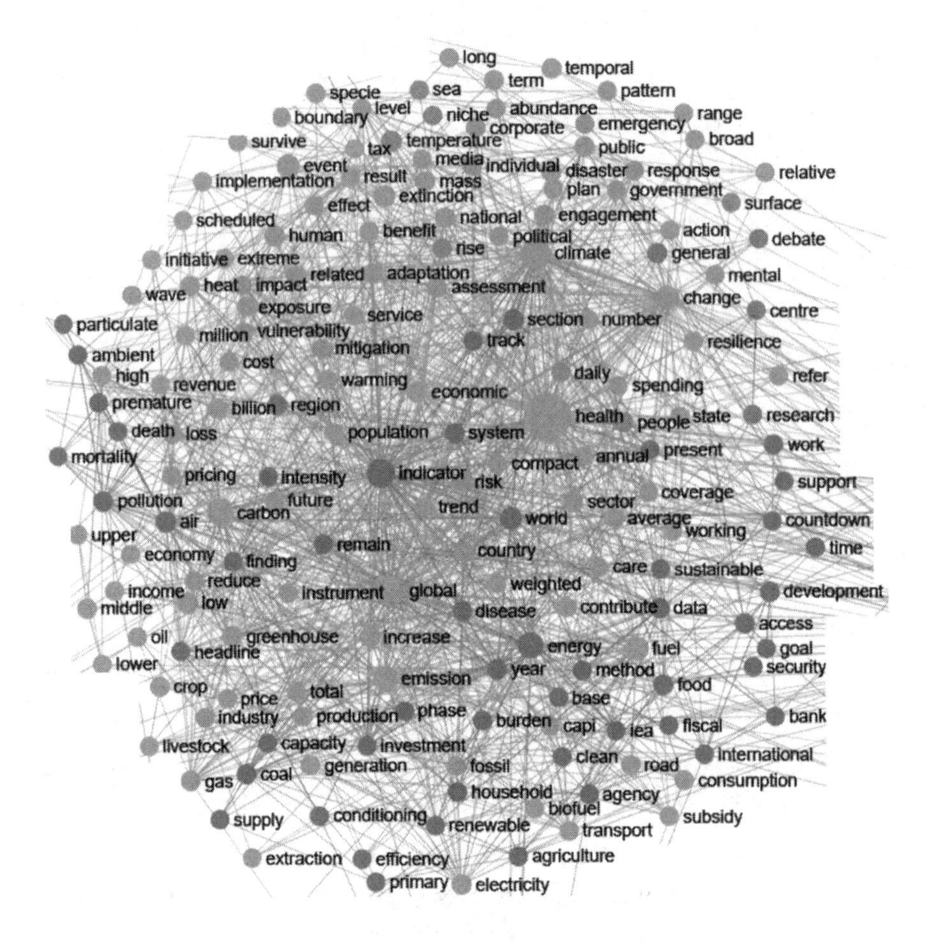

Discourse Structure Analysis

Future of the Human Climate Niche—Chu et al, PNAS 2020

The 2019 Report of the Lancet Countdown on Health and Climate Change—Lancet 2019

Bibliography and Notes

**AR6 Summary for Policy Makers—IPCC 2021*
**AR6 Technical Summary—IPCC 2021*
**AR5 Synthesis Report—IPCC 2014*
**Climate Change & Land—IPCC Special Report 2019*
**The Ocean & Cryosphere in a Changing Climate—IPCC Special Report 2019*
**Global Assessment on Biodiversity and Ecosystem Services—IPBES 2019*
**The Public Inquiry into the Piper Alpha Disaster: —HMSO 1990*
**Piper Alpha Survivors & Relatives—Public testimony*
**Global Report on Internal Displacement 2019—IDMC*
**International Migration 2019—UN Dep. Of Economic & Social Affairs*
**Cabinet Papers associated with the Piper Alpha Disaster 1988*
**Climate Change 2014—IPCC WGII 2014*
**Theses of History IX—Walter Benjamin (1940)*
**The Origins of Fossil Capital: From Water to Steam in the British Cotton Industry, Andreas Malm, Historical Materialism 25.1 (2013)*
**The Responsibility to Prepare & Prevent: A climate security governance framework for 21st c.—2019*
**A Security threat Assessment of Global Climate Change—National Security, Military & Intelligence Panel on Climate Change 2020*
**A Climate Security Plan for America—The Climate Security & Advisory Group 2019*
**Future of the human climate niche—Chu et al, PNAS 2020*
**The 2019 report of The Lancet Countdown on health and climate change—Lancet 2019*

Acknowledgements

As always...where to start?

I am truly grateful for the friends and mentors who have supported and encouraged me in the development of this collection. Especial thanks to Elizabeth Rimmer, my editor, to Imogen Stirling who provided insight and coaching in the early stages of development of this work and to Sheila Wakefield, Founder and Editor at Red Squirrel Press for her continuing support and enthusiasm.

My warmest thanks to Aileen Ackland, Ashley Milne & Judith Taylor who read and listened at various stages of the development and offered advice and encouragement and to Hamish Napier and Mark Thomson who offered wisdom in the musical and performance aspects of *Pibroch.*

Thanks are due also to the editors of the following publications in which a number of these poems first appeared: *Northwords Now*, *Earthlines* by the Edinburgh Geological Society and *Climate Matters* by Riptide Press.

And thank you, as always, to Gerry Cambridge for turning my words into a book in his characteristically insightful and meticulous ways.

A Note on Textual Analysis Techniques Used

The development of this collection has made extensive use of the Infranodus Network Analysis tool to interrogate very large bodies of text such as those listed in the bibliography. This involved the analysis of large volumes of textual data to identify key concepts and, perhaps more importantly, terms within these key texts and bodies of testimony. The approach allowed bias and nuance in the discussion and lived experience of catastrophe to be explored poetically against a rigorous framework.

A NOTE ON THE TYPE

This book is set in Foundry Wilson, a redrawing of a 1760 font from Scottish type founder Alexander Wilson (1714–1786), a polymath who from 1760 to 1786 was the University of Glasgow's first Regius Professor of Astronomy. Many of Wilson's typefaces were produced exclusively for the Foulis brothers' classics published by Glasgow University Press. Foundry Wilson is a highly distinctive and robust serif typeface which functions excellently in a digital environment.